Make Light Work
10 Tools for Inner Knowing

KATE SUTHERLAND

INCITE
P R E S S

VANCOUVER, CANADA

Incite Press
4101 Main Street, Box 74026
Vancouver, British Columbia
Canada, V5V 5C8
604-838-1406
incitepress@telus.net
www.makelightwork.org

ORDERING INFORMATION

Quantity Sales. Special discounts are available on quantity purchases. Contact Incite Press for details.

Individual Sales. Request the book directly through your local book store, or order online, either through Amazon or MakeLightWork.org.

Customized Sales. Contact Incite Press if you are interested in a customized version of Make Light Work – e.g. for students, frontline workers, emerging leaders, etc. Co-branding is possible.

Developmental Editor: Saskia Wolsak. Copy Editor: AAA WordSmith Documentation Services. Cover and interior illustrations: Helen D'Souza. Cover design: Frances Ishii. Text design: Tamara MacKenzie.

Printed in the United States. First Edition.

Library and Archives Canada Cataloguing in Publication

Sutherland, Kate, 1957-
    Make light work : 10 tools for inner knowing / Kate Sutherland.

Includes bibliographical references.
ISBN 978-0-9866127-0-1

    1. Consciousness. 2. Intuition. 3. Insight. I. Title.

BF311.S817 2010   153   C2010-903698-0

Dedicated to quickening peace and joy for you,
and everything you are connected to.

Cover Art

Artist, Helen D'Souza, sees intuition as offering each of us something akin to an inner GPS (global positioning system) to help us navigate through life. The diamond shape speaks to the four directions of a compass. The diamond also symbolizes the third eye, or seat of wisdom. In the center is the sun icon, a metaphor for the light of our inner essence, and a shape that evokes the iris of an eye. Radiating outward from the sun are hands that turn inner knowing into action, and express how, "Many hands make light work."

CONTENTS

Introduction

This is a book about easier ways of doing things. It comes from my twenty years' experience with what I call inner work tools – tools that can help you live and work in ways that are more effective, more in harmony with your true self, and more fun.

Inner work means ways of working that are interior – based in intuition, consciousness, intention, and perspective. It does not replace logical thinking, practical know-how, or scientific knowledge. Rather, it complements them with the insights that come when we stop and listen for our inner wisdom.

The inner work tools in this book are my top ten – the ones I use daily and weekly in my personal and professional life. I apply them to tasks, projects, relationships, decisions, challenging circumstances, and new opportunities. In my experience, they are as practical for living wisely and well as hammers and saws are for building a house.

If you read a chapter and it does not appeal to you, I hope you will look further. The tools are very different, and they are relevant to different types of situations. I believe there is something here for you; something that can help you live the life you are meant to be living.

First hint

The seed that has grown into this book germinated in my teens. I was sixteen years old and working on a project involving wood, precise measurements, and clean angles. There was no one else in the workshop and I had been fumbling and figuring for over an hour; I was frustrated almost to the point of tears.

Then Claude strolled in, the hip youth mentor from Quebec. In seconds he sized up the situation and said with compassionate gentleness:

> *If you are having difficulties,*
> *stop, and look for an easier way.*

He handed me a tool I had never seen before.

I do not remember what I was building or what the tool was. What has stayed with me was how my world changed in that moment. I "got" that life doesn't have to be difficult. I knew in my bones the importance of stopping to regroup when things get challenging – to pause, to ask for help, or to find a new approach. And I gained a deep appreciation for practical tools.

The other core insight

Sixteen years later, in 1990, my ongoing search for better ways of working took me to the Findhorn Foundation, an educational center in Northern Scotland. That is where I was first introduced to the concept of *inner work*, and to five of the tools in this book.

Here is the story of my first introduction to this way of working. It distills the whole of the book into one sentence, and in many ways captures all you need to know.

In 1990, I had been working on social change projects for many years, loving the meaningful work and wonderful colleagues until two crushing disappointments pulled the plug. Devastated and burned out, I began looking even more intently for ways of working that are win-win-win for individuals, for communities, and for the planet.

I arrived at the Findhorn Foundation's Cluny Hill College on April 21, tired, bruised, and confused. There was a long line at registration, so instead of checking in right away, I stepped outside into a stunning spring day. The grounds were beautiful. From the hill top, I could see silvery ancient beeches, daffodils, and lush green grass. The warm sun and soft breezes were like a soothing balm. I didn't have to rush anymore. I could be with myself, stopped, for the first time in years.

I wandered, exploring this new place. And then out of the blue, I heard a voice inside my head as if spoken aloud:

Everything you need is inside.

Perhaps a better description is that the voice came out of left field. I had never experienced anything like this before (and only twice since). The authority of the voice was profound. It came into my awareness not as something alien that I needed to evaluate, but as bedrock truth. Pure intuitive knowing.

And then I smiled: I could go home now. I had received what I had come for. I understood that the words spoken were the essence of a different way of working, and all I needed to do was unpack the gift.

Receiving gifts

I do not know about you, but I am not always great at receiving gifts. It can take me years to integrate a new item of clothing into my regular wardrobe, though I shake my head looking back when it later becomes a favourite, worn to shreds and mourned when it dies.

So while I knew that the voice answered my quest, I also knew I needed help to integrate its wisdom into my life. I needed support to envision what I would be doing and being come Monday morning.

Like many before me who planned to visit the Findhorn Foundation for a week or two, I ended up living at that intentional community for several years. In its supportive embrace, I learned a different way of working, one centered in clarity of purpose and alignment with that purpose, and one that helped me journey from living in my head to greater self-love and better balance of heart and mind.

How I made these shifts was in very large part through regular use of the tools in this book. You see, the practices in this book have worked *on* me as much as they have worked *for* me. Just as regularly swinging a hammer would strengthen muscles in my arm, daily inner work has strengthened my faith, trust, intuition, and alignment with purpose. The way I see myself has changed, along with the way I see the world.

Going inside

My deep faith is that the answers to life's questions big and small are inside for each of us – both as individuals, and when we access "group mind[1]". At some level, each of us knows what matters – what is good and true, and our part of the way forward.

---

1 A discussion of collective intelligence and group wisdom is beyond the scope of this book. Using inner work approaches in group contexts can be very powerful. Suggestions for how to use these tools in groups are forthcoming at www.KateRSutherland.com.

But too often we have forgotten what we know, not listened to the whispers and nudges, or been too enthralled by the whirl of modern life to recognize signs. Many of us do not know how to gain access to inner knowing and, lacking practice, have little trust in what comes from within.

In my experience, this can change quickly. I have worked with men and women from all walks of life – from residents of Canada's poorest postal code to executives, from teenagers to seniors, from government and business people to community members.

In a matter of minutes, and across sectors and situations, a simple exercise allows people to tap into potent personal images and insights. Usually there is some degree of apprehension at first. Some fidget or ask questions, dancing at the edge of this new (old) world. Then, in group after group, people relax once they experience inner work. For most, it is like coming home.

Inner knowing is immediately accessible and available 24/7. I hope you will receive its gifts by finding inner work approaches that work for you, and doing what it takes to integrate them into your life. And it is important to honour the inner work you already do.

Using this book

Each chapter introduces a tool. I suggest you start by exploring all the options. Give yourself permission to experience each one.

I recommend reading Groundwork (see page 19) sooner rather than later. This chapter introduces the *being* side of inner work. As the name suggests, groundwork is crucial to create a strong foundation for using the tools, and it will help you get the most out of your inner work.

The final chapter shares how I use inner work throughout a day, and offers ideas for mixing and matching the different tools. It is designed to answer the key questions: Where do I start? What do I do Monday morning?

My intention is to offer a book you might dip into over and over – any time you need reminding that it doesn't have to be difficult, and any time you need a nudge to access the answers within. At these times, you can use the Tool Guide (see page 99). This one page overview matches tools with specific situations, such as relationships, decision-making, and starting new initiatives. You can also refer to the quick reminders listed in the Even Lighter section on page 89.

Sharing what works

There are many forms of inner work and most of us already have ways of gaining access to our inner knowing. My husband's insights come through meditation and soaking in the tub; one friend gains understanding from her dreams; another friend solves problems as she paints water colours. Exercising or being in nature is often part of "Aha!" moments.

In recent years, I have encountered greater openness to inner work. Where I once used the tools without telling clients or colleagues, I now share what I am doing and find people are open and curious. By telling friends and colleagues about approaches that work for you, you can help widen the circle of people intentionally accessing their inner knowing.

You can share stories, resources, suggestions, and questions in the blog and discussion forums at www.KateRSutherland.com. The website also has resources to help you convene or join face-to-face circles where people gather weekly or biweekly to support each other to integrate inner work into their lives. See Further Resources on page 90.

Setting an intention

To get the most from a book like this, it can be helpful to name a specific goal, purpose, or intention you hope to achieve by reading it. It could be that you seek guidance about major changes or new opportunities. It might be that you want more of a particular quality in your life, such as joy, peace, or creativity.

Pause for a moment, and allow an intention to emerge. Trust yourself to know what is best for you, and have fun!

1
Automatic Writing

Automatic writing is a way to tap into your inner knowing and make it visible through written words on a page. The word "automatic" does not mean I go into a trance, or feel as if my hand is being moved for me. The key distinction is getting beyond the personality level to a place of deeper wisdom and insight.

Automatic writing was the first inner work tool I used on a daily basis. It changed my life, helping me release negative patterns and shift my world view. It has remained a favourite tool, like a great cooking knife – effective, efficient, and useful for all sorts of situations.

Before learning automatic writing, I had been a regular journal writer. In my teens and twenties, I filled volumes to sort my way through emotional turmoil and challenging circumstances.

Then in October 1990, as part of becoming a staff member of the Findhorn Foundation, I was introduced to automatic writing. I instantly appreciated its power and potential. This wonderful tool quickly took me to a level of clarity I had previously only occasionally reached after an hour or more of regular journaling.

Looking back, I am very grateful for what happened next, because although it is one thing to learn about a great tool, it is another to integrate it into your life.

Getting started

Later that October day, I was sitting at a dining room table in the Community Center, writing in my journal. After several pages of typical writing, I suddenly tapped into a deeper clarity. The way I shaped letters became smooth and even:

> *"You need to have a daily practice, and you need to start*
> *that practice now. Close your eyes and meditate until*
> *you know what that daily practice will be."*

My impression of this "voice" was utterly positive. So I closed my eyes and turned inward.

Moments later I "got" the idea of doing 20 minutes of automatic writing first thing each day for a year. The new regimen would be both a stretch and a perfectly customized program. I liked writing, and 20 minutes felt just right for my first daily practice. Then and there I made the commitment.

Here is what I was taught about automatic writing, seasoned with tips I have learned along the way:

AUTOMATIC WRITING

1. **Find a time and a place where you will not be disturbed.** Do whatever is necessary to ensure you will not be interrupted.

2. **Have pen and paper ready.** Pick a pen you like, and one that allows you to write quickly. Have writing materials close at hand, but not in your hands or lap.

3. **Sit quietly and relax.** It is best to sit with your back and neck straight, with both feet on the ground if you are using a chair. If you wear glasses, consider taking them off as a way of shifting your attention inwards. Close your eyes. Bring your awareness to your body and take time to relax in a way that works for you. For example, pay attention to your breath, tense and release tight muscles from toes to head, or imagine you are in a hot bath. Do not rush; take time at this stage as it helps you to go deeper later. With practice, you will know when to go on to the next step.

4. **Turn your attention inward.** There are many ways to do this, and sometimes I use a combination of two or three:

   o Visualize your work space, and see yourself put all the papers and busyness off to one side.

   o Imagine going to a place in nature that has special meaning for you, and pay close attention to what you see, smell, hear, and feel.

   o "Tune in" to your heart, and focus your attention on your chest area (the heart chakra) until you are aware of its glowing radiant energy.

   o Ask silently, "May the cares and busyness of every-day life move to the side, and may my attention turn inwards, to my center, to my place of wisdom, peace and joy."

The most important thing is that you hold a clear intention in your mind and heart to connect with your inner wisdom.

5. **Invoke the highest.** Using unspoken words that work for you, ask that everything that comes through you serves the highest good for all concerned. For more information on how to do this, see Groundwork (page 19).

6. **Clarify your purpose or intention.** What is it you seek insight into? If you have a specific issue or concern, ask for insights. Then invite your divine/higher/essential self to respond. You can also experiment with open questions like, "What am I not paying enough attention to?" "What is it that wants to unfold through me/us/this context?"

7. **Write.** When you have even the tiniest glimmer of something coming to you, write it down. Continue writing whatever comes into your mind quickly and without censoring yourself. If you get stuck, keep your pen moving by repeating the last sentence or phrase. If what comes is not clear or raises other questions, ask for clarity or further insights. Write until you run dry, and write a bit more as a way of overcoming inner resistance. You may find the extra time takes you through surface issues to deeper concerns and deeper wisdom.

8. **Act on what you get.** It is simple: if you listen to your inner voice, it will share its abundant insight. If you ignore what it brings to your attention, you will cut off the flow. For this reason, it is important to ask for insights only about things that you are ready to act on.

9. **Write often.** Automatic writing is a way of having a closer relationship with the part of you that is wise, whole, and authentic. Like any relationship, it needs time to develop trust, intimacy, and a shared history that is the basis for going deeper. The more you write and experience the benefits it brings you, the more confidence you will have in your own inner voice. If it

suits you, 5-20 minutes of automatic writing is a wonderful daily practice.

Finer points

- You may wish to use a journal or binder that is dedicated exclusively to automatic writing since it can be insightful and interesting to look back on what you have written. Picking one without lines allows more freedom for the size of your writing to vary.

- If you are normally a good speller, be curious if you make a spelling mistake: sometimes you may be blocking a deeper truth. As soon as you notice the mistake, drop any possible self-criticism and free-associate with the misspelling – playfully, quickly, spontaneously – to see if you can uncover what it is about.

- The more emotional or agitated you are about a topic, the more you need to be vigilant that you are truly tuning into your inner wisdom. I recommend leaving "hot" topics alone until you become more familiar with the texture of your inner voice.

- You can experiment with different ways of using automatic writing. For example, I have used automatic writing to give voice to images from my dreams, things I have misplaced, and objects that catch my attention as I glance around a room (see Unpacking Flirts, page 27). You can also write dialogues between your personality level and your inner wisdom. This allows you to ask questions and share responses to the insights you are getting. You can dialogue with a part of your body, a comfort food, a lost wallet, an inner guide (see Inner Guides, page 63) – just about anything.

- You might be tempted to have an inner dialogue with your boss or partner. I recommend waiting until you have solid experience with automatic writing before tuning into another person where stakes are high – the likelihood of ego interference is just too great.

- Try writing with your non-dominant hand (left hand if you are right-handed, and vice versa). I find these writings especially profound. They have a simplicity and directness that gets to the core.

- The content of what you write may challenge you to embrace perspectives and possibilities that seem too good to be true. This is a good thing. We can be so attached to drama and struggle that one of the biggest questions most of us face is, *"How much joy, grace, and ease can I accept?"*

My first year

Integrating 20 minutes of automatic writing into each day was both a stretch and a perfect fit, like Cinderella's slipper. I gave myself the flexibility of writing later in the day, and of missing occasionally, but by and large I kept a regular "first thing" schedule.

Even though I believe there is great value in committing for, say, a year, to any new practice, the crucial part is to take the first step, then the next, then the next. Slowly but surely, the amazing progress you experience will encourage you to continue.

What I remember most from those early days was how much automatic writing challenged my sense of self. I had grown up getting straight A's and driven to achieve, yet underneath was a negative core belief that I was not good enough.

The writing helped me access an inner voice that spoke with clarity and authority, and it had deep appreciation for who I was. It would address me as Sweet Kate, and saw me as essentially good. It honoured small things I had done – things that were often a tiny portion of my awareness or activity – and point to them as embodying an authentic way of being in the world.

Day after day, my inner voice invited me to have a life full of success, joy, peace, and happiness. I remember feeling such a possibility was too good to be true. But my inner voice would respond, *"Doubt is toxic; doubt kills new possibilities,"* and suggest I suspend my resistance and pay attention to the results that were coming in my life.

This was difficult for me, so it was like an exquisitely customized workshop to have the writing respond to every thought and defence, at the exact moment they crossed my mind.

I tussled with doubt for months, not able to fully trust. Over time, the peace, clarity, and excellent guidance of my inner voice gradually won me over. By the end of the first year, I had developed significant confidence that the good news was for real.

Other benefits

Besides improving my sense of self, automatic writing helped me learn what I call the *texture* of inner alignment. Through reflecting on my daily practice – and especially the times I misspelled words – I was able to distinguish when I was clearly on track with my inner voice, and when there was interference. It was like homing in on a radio channel; I could connect to my "guidance system" with greater and greater ease.

Another great benefit was becoming more intuitive, not just during the writing practice but all through the day. What happened, as I understand it, is that daily practice cultivated

A sample

Here is automatic writing I did while writing this book, including a typical opening endearment and feedback on my process.

Dearest Katalia,

Do not try so hard. You have a natural voice that is plenty good enough. Let your writing flow. You are writing!

I want to come through: there is a voice inside every person that can guide and support. This is higher self or inner wisdom or wise being. It is the basis of Assagioli's work[2] and of all forms of guided meditation.

The inner voice is both personal and impersonal.

Personal in that it reflects intimate knowing of every iota of personal thoughts, feelings, sensations, and aspirations. Impersonal in the sense it is founded in the whole, and profoundly not attached to "small self" considerations.

This voice cuts through everything extraneous and frequently elevates core principles and patterns neglected by distracted personalities.

It is a superb guide – exquisitely tailored, moment by moment, to the unfolding in each and every person.

For some, this voice manifests as lyrics from popular songs. For others, it is sensations and intimations; for others words spoken or written like this. All different access points but the same source: inner knowing.

---

2 For an introduction to Roberto Assagioli's approach called Psychosynthesis, please see Further Resources on page 90.

the muscle of inner listening the way sit-ups cultivate strong posture.

The real proof of the pudding, however, was in the eating. Automatic Writing had major impact on all dimensions of my life: relationships, work, conflict situations, peace of mind, health. The more I allowed the writing's wisdom to touch my heart, the more it deepened, and the more my life improved.

If you are willing to receive its gifts, I believe Automatic Writing will be of similar benefit to you.

Groundwork

Groundwork sets the conditions for doing inner work. It is the preparation you need to do to get the most out of using the tools in this book. Think of it as laying a foundation. Without a strong foundation, inner work can lead you astray. With a strong foundation, you can trust the insights and input you get through your inner work.

Groundwork does not take much time. What it does require is putting attention on things we usually ignore, the way a fish does not see the water it swims in.

Seeing the water we swim in

As a kid, my favourite museum was the local Science Center, and one of the best parts was the Arcade, a huge gallery of games and activities that taught science through play. Every time I was there, I delighted in the optical illusions, seeing first a hag and then a beautiful woman, or first faces, then a vase, and back to faces.

What I loved was the way optical illusions revealed how choice is at the heart of what we see. In the image shown here, do you focus on what is black, or what is white?

If you see the black faces, then white is the ground of what you see, and you miss seeing the vase. If instead you see the white vase, then black is ground for you, and you miss seeing there are two people almost nose to nose. Both are valid ways of seeing, but in our day-to-day living, we tend to miss seeing "the ground" because we are focused only on what scientists of perception call "the figure".

What if optical illusions were not special cases? What if, for example, we balanced our society's emphasis on doing (the figure) with more attention to how we are being (the ground)? What if we trained ourselves to see both the "figure" and the "ground" in all situations?

Telling the whole story

Early in writing this book, wanting to share the inner work I do (the figure), I realized I must simultaneously share the quality of being (the ground) I bring to it. I need to share the whole picture: both the faces and the vase. Otherwise, it would be like sharing a recipe that was missing key ingredients.

What I *do* is use the tools outlined in this book. The quality of *being* I bring to them stems from *awareness*, *intention*, and *openness*. These are the three essential elements of laying a strong foundation.

Before using any inner work tools I always establish "the ground" in these three ways. Here is how:

GROUNDWORK

1. Center through self awareness

If awareness is like a lamp, we tend to spend most of our time illuminating things, people, and ideas around us, and very little time shining light on ourselves.

The moment I bring awareness to my breath, or to my shoulders, or to my core (the solar plexus), it is as if I snap back "home". Other ways to become centered are to meditate, do yoga, chant, sing, go for a walk, or spend time with a tree. Pausing for a moment and simply intending to be centered works too.

Being self-aware is synonymous with being centered, even if one is emotionally agitated. Being centered is a key part of the foundation for effective inner work.

2. Set intention

Once I am centered, I set an overarching intention:

> *"May everything that comes*
> *through me serve the highest."*

You might say serve God or Gaia, or Truth or Love – whatever words work for you. Sometimes I say, *"May I be in service of what wants to come through."*

Saying or thinking either phrase immediately shifts my center of gravity away from ego-driven, small "s" self to big "S" Self, a point of awareness that is interconnected with all that is. It is like flipping a railway

An invitation

I invite you to take a moment and dedicate your reading to serving the highest (or whatever language works for you).

Then notice what you notice!

switch to take small "s" self off-line and activate big "S" Soul. I know I have flipped that switch when I feel aligned – as if I have just had a great session with a chiropractor.

As I see it, being aligned and serving the highest are two sides of the same coin, and they both require me to be true to my authentic self. Alignment means that I am living my purpose, and that my actions, words, thoughts, and energy fulfill my part in the whole.

At the same time, I am mindful that I cannot know what it is that serves the highest. I must approach each situation with humility because my perspective is inevitably limited. Setting intention is a way of asking that I be guided by life and by inner work to what is truly of service.

3. Open

After setting intention, the next step is to become open or receptive.

Moment by moment, like clams in a tide pool, we open and close our "shells" – sometimes open, for example, to learning from what a friend has to say, and other times not.

Inner work involves opening to our inner wisdom and truth, to another perspective. We only benefit from inner work tools if we are open to the gifts they bring us. Put another way, I do not engage in inner work unless I am committed to acting on what I get.

So this step involves a moment in which I check within to make sure I am open to insights, and that I trust enough to commit to act on what I get. I have found it helpful to tap into my faith and trust that this is a safe and wonderful thing to do.

Here I often think of a question posed years ago by my brother, Stephen Sutherland: "Is the universe your lover or your betrayer?" I think many of us have a foot in each camp. Before using inner work tools, my practice is to "center" myself in the camp where I see the universe as my lover.

If you are a person who sees the universe as neither a friend or a foe, neither good nor evil, the core of this step remains: choose to open to and trust your inner knowing.

In summary

In doing this groundwork, it is as though I am adjusting three inner dials: first to centered awareness, second to serving the highest, and third to opening to trust. This ground then creates a spaciousness in which I am far more able to integrate the input from different inner work tools.

For me, groundwork is a crucial form of inner work, and the most fundamental shift each of us can make. If I had to choose between doing the groundwork and using the tools, I would choose groundwork every time. The benefits are so profound.

Thankfully, there is no need to choose. We can have both: lay the ground for inner work AND receive the benefit of inner work tools for decisions, project planning, event organizing, relationship quandaries – you name it.

Figure of Eight Breathing

If you want to center deeply and quickly, try this exercise.

a. Optional: take off eyeglasses, any heavy jewellery, and footwear made of rubber or plastic.

b. Stand with your feet shoulder-width apart, eyes closed, and your attention on your breath. Sitting or lying down works too, but standing is the easiest way to start.

c. Inhale slowly and bring your awareness to your heart.

d. Exhale slowly and imagine your breath is traveling down the front of your body and penetrating to the center of the Earth.

e. Inhale slowly and imagine you are drawing energy up from the center of the Earth, up the back of your body, and into your heart.

f. Exhale slowly and imagine that your breath is going from your heart up the front of your body as high as it can go – to the Ether, the stars, heaven – whatever works for you.

g. Inhale slowly and imagine you are drawing energy down from above, down the back of your body and into your heart.

h. Repeat this "figure of eight" as long as feels right – perhaps 5-20 cycles at the beginning. When you are familiar with this practice, 4 or 5 cycles is enough to feel quite grounded.

To start, I suggest tracing the figure of eight shape with one hand, as a way to help your awareness move.

For other ways to increase receptivity, see the Becoming Receptive sidebar on page 29.

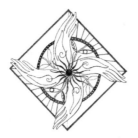

2
Unpacking Flirts

One the simplest forms of inner work starts with noticing what you notice. What catches your attention as you go about your day? How does what you notice relate to a current question, issue, or task? If you are open and attentive, answers and information can be right under your nose.

Arnold Mindell, founder of Process Oriented Psychology, coined the term "flirt" to describe this process. He says that, like our night-time dreams, flirts offer potent answers and insights into our questions and growing edges. I love the term *flirt* because it captures the subtlety of the cues: was that a signal, or am I just imagining it?

If you are like me, grocery shopping can be a great training ground in recognizing flirts. I have learned to pay closer attention to the way certain things catch my eye as I move through the aisles. I used to ignore or discount subtle signals, but I always regretted it when I had to go out again for some staple or key ingredient.

Not everything you notice is a flirt, but with practice, you can learn what a true flirt feels like. Here is how to do it.

UNPACKING FLIRTS

1. Have a question or intention in mind.

2. Center and ground. For more on this, see the Groundwork chapter, page 19.

3. Dedicate the inner work by asking in your own way that it serve the highest. Be sure you always do this step. It is what takes you beyond the personality level into alignment with your core purpose.

4. Become receptive (see sidebar), and invite answers and input relevant to your question or intention.

5. Scan your environment, noticing when something catches your attention – either immediately, or over the next while. Flirts can be one thing, a bunch of things, a quality, or a sound. Sometimes they "jump off the shelf," and call our attention in no uncertain terms. Sometimes a flirt is subtle, a barely perceptible signal.

6. Trust that the first thing you notice is a great something to work with.

7. Open to the insights the flirt has to offer. You might free associate, paying attention to what comes into your mind when you focus on the flirt. You can also use the tools Automatic Writing, Inner Guides, and Coin Toss to explore the flirt's meaning.

Finer points

• Working with this tool cultivates a way of seeing and being. Over time, working with flirts becomes less structured and more integrated. You simply pay attention to the things

Becoming receptive

Try one or two of these approaches:

- Relax your body, especially your shoulders, jaw, buttocks, and eyes.

- Soften your gaze, shifting from the more normal "spotlight" visual focus to a "floodlight" focus that includes what is in the periphery of your vision.

- Focus on your breath for 2-3 breaths or until you become fully present.

- Set personality aside, perhaps by imagining you are clearing a desk, or closing a door.

- Soften the focus of your awareness in order to connect to your body at the energetic level. For this, it can be helpful to start in the heart area and then extend your awareness to include your whole energy body.

- Simply ask that you become receptive – the intention to be receptive increases receptivity.

that catch your attention, and how they relate to current intentions, issues, or tasks.

- Any practice that helps you be more receptive enhances the effectiveness of working with flirts. Meditation, exercise, and yoga are obvious examples. Getting your energy moving by dancing or singing is another. And receptivity tends to be heightened just before sleep and on waking.

- Sometimes what catches my attention is a series of related or similar signals. If I notice something three times in a day or week, I take that to be a flirt, even if I do not have a question or challenge I am working with at the time.

- I frequently use decks of cards as a "flirt" system, using one of my personal favourites of the many decks available at spiritual or new age book stores. After following steps 1-4 in the above practice, I draw a card. The card tells me what quality to bring to my situation or intention. For example, I recently drew "Effectiveness" as a guide for a troubling professional relationship. It instantly helped me orient to the outcomes we both want, to trust our common ground, and snapped me out of feeling, "I can't work with this woman." A two minute activity cut through what could have been hours of interpersonal process!

- A lovely way to work with flirts is to go out into nature. While human-made environments are rich, flirts from the natural world seem to mainline into a deeper place in the psyche.

- Going with the first thing you notice is likely to yield the richest results. The temptation can be to reject a flirt as silly, or unacceptable, or "not me." My favourite story about this was my mother's experience at a personal growth workshop decades ago. She was asked to go outside for a walk and to bring back something sacred. The first thing that called her attention was a rusty pop can. She rejected it immediately, but as she continued on her walk, nothing else was right. In tears, she returned to the pop can, gaining in the process a new level of self-acceptance. She saw that everything is sacred, even what she most rejected about herself.

Possible pitfalls

Paying attention to signs and signals can sometimes descend into seeing everything as bad or good omens. This is not helpful. If you get caught in this way, teach yourself the difference between tapping into knowledge and tapping into fear. The "texture" (how it feels in your body) is different. In general, if there is fear or anxiety in the mix, it is not a flirt.

A story

A flirt helped me with a crisis-cum-turning-point in my relationship.

I had gone with my partner, Evan, for a winter retreat to Iona, the tiny and beautiful island on the west coast of Scotland. I do not remember how it started, but I played out my hysterical drama-queen pattern so forcefully it became the last straw: Evan ended the relationship. His clarity was so final, there was nothing to do but pack my bags and set out to find other accommodation.

I took the short ferry ride to the Isle of Mull and found a room in the fourth and last Bed & Breakfast in town. I remember a brown bedspread, cream-coloured walls, and close-sloping ceilings. Alone and heartbroken, I replayed the final scenes with feelings of deep regret.

At dinner, I poured out my story to Dick and Dave, the only other guests at the B&B. The two were travelling carpet salesmen and as salt-of-the-earth as their sheep-farmer customers.

"Yuu haff to go back, Katie! Aach! Yuu haff to go back!" said Dave, peering at me through coke-bottle glasses.

What stopped me was the fear that I would keep creating hissy fits. I had no proof for myself or Evan that I could change.

Later that night I wrote page after page of sadness and despair. Then, out of the corner of my eye, I noticed a monarch butterfly fluttering around the room.

It was a flirt I could not miss. Dick and Dave had been surreal. But to see a butterfly inside the B&B, in the middle of a heavy rain storm, in the middle of December, in the middle of Scotland blew open my understanding of reality.

I used automatic writing to tune in to what the butterfly had to say. Its core message: not only is fundamental and transformative change possible, such change is the very fabric of life.

I needed to hear this many times and in many ways to be able to let it in fully. When the shift happened a part of me knew, without being able to say how, that I was not going to play out the pattern anymore.

Even so, it took every ounce of courage to go back to Iona the next day. As I walked down a country road, who but Evan crested a hill to walk toward me. We met on neutral territory, he had had several minutes warning, and the opportunity to turn the other way.

Long story short: we reconnected AND I never again played out the pattern that had previously run in a predictable, highly destructive groove.

Whether seeking help with a relationship crisis or with grocery shopping, paying attention to flirts offers specific and helpful insights, and a pathway to a stronger connection to your inner knowing.

3
Setting the Energy

We are setting the energy all the time, most often unconsciously. Common settings are drudgery, struggle, effort, and conflict. We expect difficulties. We "hate meetings", or family gatherings, or our everyday work situations.

It is like a bad joke: we set energy for "struggle" or "conflict", and then confirm negative beliefs about our "reality".

Other times, we set out to have fun, or an adventure, or success. When we are getting together with great friends, we *know* we will have a good time. Or, if we are confident of our welding/cooking/you-name-it skills, then sure enough, everything turns out just right.

The tool I call Setting the Energy is about bringing conscious choice to the energies you want to experience. Just as you select what clothes to wear, you can choose what qualities infuse your day, task, or project.

Pausing at the start

Most mornings, I take a few minutes to set the energy for the day, taking advantage of the in-between moments after waking and before getting out of bed. Recently in the midst of a busy period, and facing another packed day, what I most wanted was to have a break. So I set the energy for fun, and had a ball. All through the day, I felt a bubbly and delighted buoyancy. I was unusually spontaneous, taking time for a walk and to connect with my daughter, and then unusually focused to get done what I needed to do – another kind of fun.

In addition to setting the energy for a whole day, I also set the energy for specific tasks. For example, when my daughter was a baby, I chose to change her diapers with the energy of love rather than resistance or disgust. The result was that a typically unpleasant task became a sacred act. Facing a long flight of stairs, I choose vitality. Getting into cold water at the swimming pool, I choose excitement. Preparing to facilitate a meeting, I choose awareness and clarity. The list is as endless as the fullness of life.

It is also possible to set the energy on a macro scale. For example, you can set the energy for a major transition like moving or starting a new job. Since the larger scale makes the stakes higher, I often tune in for guidance about how best to set the energy, most often using Coin Toss, Automatic Writing, or Guiding Image.

In all its forms, setting the energy is like planting a seed. It involves faith that the tiny speck you put into the earth will sprout and grow. I hope that after you have a bit of experience with setting the energy, you too will have faith in this way of working, and reap abundant benefits from what you sow.

Here is how to do it.

SETTING THE ENERGY

1. Pause at the beginning of a new day, activity, or project, and take a few breaths to bring yourself present.

2. Dedicate your inner work to serving the highest.

3. Connect with your purpose for the day, activity, or project.

4. Choose how you would like things to go, naming the qualities. You might also tune in about what qualities want to come through you.

5. "Run the energy" of these qualities. For example, if you are setting energy to work creatively, take a few moments to connect to the energy of creativity. You might recall a time when you felt creative. What were the body sensations? Feel them now, and invite them to flow into every part of your body, and to fill the room and the tools and processes you are engaging with.

6. Let go and trust that, "As you have sown, so shall you reap."

Finer points

- It is great to experiment. Try setting energy before an important phone call or conversation, before meetings and presentations, at the start of a new project, and before making love. (It took me 18 years to think of this last application, and I highly recommend it!)

- How you set your energy, consciously or unconsciously, ripples out to affect people and events around you. For example, if you are facilitating a meeting, the way you set your energy will help to bring the same energy into the group. We influence one another, the way iron filings are pulled and pushed by the force field around a magnet. In my experience, this field effect is particularly strong around people in leadership positions.

• Setting energy on a regular basis helps us notice and name our addiction to drama, difficulty, problems, etc. The ego does not let go easily when we choose love over fear, ease over struggle, joyous flow over stuckness. Patient repetition and just noticing resistance when it is present helps to dissolve it.

• To reset energy in the midst of an emotional storm, try repeating this simple sequence, thanks to Thich Nhat Hanh[3]:

> *Breathing in, I calm my body.*
> *Breathing out, I smile.*
> *Dwelling in the present moment,*
> *I know this is a wonderful moment.*

• Setting energy is similar to setting an intention. Both involve making a conscious choice, and both are powerful ways to influence what happens. A classic example is setting an intention to find a parking spot. People who do this generally succeed. When setting any such specific intention, I believe it is crucial to set a prior intention to be of service to the highest. What we want at the personality level may not meet that criteria. That said, by starting with a phrase like, "If it serves the highest, ...", I feel free to intend all sorts of things.

---

3 Reprinted from *Being Peace* (1987, 2005) by Thich Nhat Hanh with permission of Parallax Press, Berkeley, California. www.parallax.org

Possible pitfalls

Watch that you do not flip this process to use it like a club on yourself when things do not go as well as you would have liked: *"I should have set energy more consciously..."*. We are always doing our best, choosing the good as we understand it.

In the test kitchen

I gained a deep appreciation of the power of setting energy through working for a year in the Kitchen Department at the Findhorn Foundation.

Each shift, the work was basically the same – preparing lunches or dinners for 150-200 people in a constantly changing team of 8-10 cooks. Each shift was led by a different member of the Kitchen Department. Lisa's shifts were always mellow. Mia's gentle and sweet. Mine were chatty and industrious. Robert's were famous for outstanding food and utter chaos.

Many factors went into these differences – like the ambitiousness of the menu and type of music playing in the kitchen – but after a year in that laboratory, I realized the best predictor was the energy of the person leading the shift.

Consciously setting the energy invites us to choose how we want things to go. It is a brief and powerful pause before we start, or re-start, that opens doors for grace and ease.

4

Muscle Testing

It's Ottawa, 1997, and I am at a restaurant I have never been to before, surveying the menu. I am with two new acquaintances, dynamic fellow participants at a professional development conference. We have bonded and are having fun.

Suddenly my attention is riveted by what my colleague is doing with her hands. It is as if she is highlighted in flourescent yellow.

"What are you doing?", I ask.

"Muscle testing what to order," she responds. She is happy to show me how she does it, and I follow her process (explained below) to choose from the menu. As it turns out I am very happy with my order, and have none of the regret I have often felt when I do not know my way around a menu.

Looking back years later, learning muscle testing has been by far the most useful take-away from that Ottawa conference.

The body knows best

Dr. David Hawkins, a psychiatrist and author, explains muscle testing by saying our bodies respond to truth and falsehood the way amoebas gravitate toward food and away from toxins. He maintains that the body tests "strong" when we speak or think something true, and tests "weak" when a statement is false.[4]

My confidence in the validity of muscle testing comes from my experience. Since my first exposure in Ottawa, I have used it daily or weekly to understand situations and to help with decisions big and small. The notion that the body registers truth rings true for me, and I have never been let down by this tool.

I hope you find it equally beneficial. Here is how to do it.

MUSCLE TESTING

1. Clarify your purpose for doing inner work.

2. Center and ground. For more on this see the Groundwork chapter at page 19.

3. Dedicate the inner work – ask in your own way that it serve the highest.

4. Prepare to muscle test (see sidebar).

5. Always confirm the appropriateness of using this tool at this time by muscle testing the following three statements (notice that these are statements, not questions):
   o I **can** use muscle testing for this issue.
   o I **may** use muscle testing for this issue.
   o I **should** use muscle testing for this issue.

---

4 For more information on how muscle testing works, see Hawkins and Diamond in Further Resources on page 90.

Getting ready to muscle test

- Drink a glass (or more) of water. Muscle testing involves the body's electrical system, which works better when you are hydrated.

- There are many ways to muscle test. Some involve two hands, some one hand, some an outstretched arm. The approach I was taught (and prefer) is:

  1. Make two interlocking rings with the thumb and index finger of each hand.

  2. Ask your body to show you what *"True"* looks like, and what *"False"* looks like. To do this, press finger and thumb together with the same firm pressure, and endeavour to pull the hands apart.

It has always been that the finger-thumb ring of my dominant hand holds strong for *"True"* such that I cannot pull my hands apart (see second image), and breaks for *"False"* (see third image). It is the opposite for some people.

- For other techniques, see John Diamond's book listed in Further Resources, or Google "muscle testing". for videos and instructions.

6. Frame your issue as a present-time statement. Do not muscle test a yes/no question, but rather whether a statement is true or false at this time. Do not muscle test about the future; muscle testing only works in the now (see Present-time sidebar).

7. Say your statement aloud or in your mind and immediately muscle test to check the truth of the statement.

8. Act on what you get!

Finer points

- Muscle testing – and inner work in general – does not replace logical thinking, practical know-how, or scientific knowledge. Different ways of knowing have different strengths. Use the approaches that best suit your needs.

- Testing simple things is a great way to build trust in this way of working. Early on, I used muscle testing to decide whether to wait for the bus or set out walking, what to order from a restaurant menu, and other minor decisions.

- As with all forms of inner work, do not test the truth of a statement unless you are prepared to act on what you get. Inner work is about coming into better alignment with what is true. When we know the truth and do not act on it, we hurt ourselves. We are better off not knowing than betraying what we know.

- I am grateful that my introduction to muscle testing stressed the importance of asking each time if it is appropriate to use the tool. My colleague impressed upon me that muscle testing is not some party trick or toy. It is not to be used for entertainment or idle curiosity. That is why the exercise above includes the process she taught me for checking appropriateness. Please use it, and pass it on if you share this tool with others.

- I occasionally get "No" when testing the appropriateness of using muscle testing for a specific issue. I notice these are times when I am testing about another person, or I am testing something for the sake of curiosity, rather than a sincere need to know.

Present-time

When my daughter was four, I used to take her for dance lessons. One time I went for a long walk in the neighbourhood as a way of passing the hour until her class was over.

I remember walking fast and far, and losing track of time. When I later glanced at my watch, I wondered what I needed to do to be sure of getting back before the class ended. My burning question was about the future, "Will I get back in time if I walk, or do I need to run?"

I reframed this question into a present-time statement: "Walking at my current pace is quick enough to get me to the class by 10:15." That was affirmed, both by muscle testing, and by life. I walked back, and still caught the final moments of the class.

You might object that rational calculations could have allowed me to reach the same conclusion in this relatively trivial instance.

For me, rational calculations go only so far toward allaying concerns relating to my daughter. By tuning in, I was able to let go of worrying – a much nicer way to arrive for the pick-up.

Remember the main point: if you have a question about something in the future, reframe it as a present-time statement.

Possible pitfalls

- Pay attention to whether you are truly open to the response being either true or false. When we have strong feelings about an issue, our ego may subtly interfere with the results. In such instances, you can structure the process so that you do not know the statement you are testing. For example, ask a friend to hold in mind one of these two statements: "Maggie is right for the job", or "Maggie is not right for the job." This way, you can do your muscle testing, and only after you have the result find out which version your friend had in mind. You can also write statements on identical cards, shuffle them, and test each one face down.

- Another common pitfall is the impulse to retest a statement, just to be sure. In my experience, retesting the same statement does not bring greater certainty but instead more confusion or doubt. Wanting to retest can be due to a lack of faith in the process or a lack of acceptance of the result. To build trust in the process, start with decisions and issues that you are willing to act on. This way, you will develop trust based on your experience of how things work out.

- Be wary of using muscle testing to justify your point of view in conversations with others. You can alienate people if muscle testing leads you to be inflexible and closed to their perspectives. I thank my daughter for her clarity on this point! While I may still go into another room to muscle test about an issue relating to her, I now take responsibility for my point of view, and express it without invoking the muscle testing result.

Making decisions

In my consulting work, most contract opportunities come through a phone call or an email. I routinely use muscle testing to decide which to accept and which to gracefully decline. Sometimes I go straight to a statement: "It serves the highest and is a high priority for me to work (or not work) on this contract." Other times, I ask for background information and feel my way into what is involved before muscle testing.

While there have been times when it took courage to turn down work, I have had enough corroboration from how things later turned out to completely trust this way of working.

Once I got a clear "No" to pursuing contract work with a friend and colleague who wanted me to join her in working on a complex job in tough community circumstances. My friend was persistent, and I muscle tested again, this time limiting my role to an initial scoping of a possible project. Getting a go-ahead, she and I had detailed conversations with the client about the goals and circumstances of the contract. These scoping conversations shed light on the situation and clarified intervention options. My part done, my colleague carried on. She later wrote me to say my initial guidance had been spot on, as she had spent many more hours on proposals and counterproposals, only to have the client back away completely from the work.

Muscle testing is wonderfully fast and easy. You can do it on the fly, anywhere. With practice, it can become an approach you use many times each day, for decisions large and small. Using this tool regularly will help you better align with serving the highest. Then, if you are like me, you will discover that being in alignment is a royal road to well-being, peace, and happiness.

5
Coin Toss

Coin Toss is a simple way to test whether a specific thought is true intuition. It gives you instant feedback, helping you learn what accurate intuition feels like in your body *right at the moment* when you are tuning in.

Over time, Coin Toss has helped me have ready access to my intuition on a daily basis, and moment by moment. I have learned, for example, that my intuition is accurate when I have a buzzing sensation at the top of my head.

Intuition is the ability to know something immediately, and without conscious reasoning or direct experience. It comes as hunches, vague feelings, or flashes of insight – stronger or weaker depending on how open and attuned we are to intuitive knowing.

My favourite example is the first time I saw the man who is now my husband. He came into the room, bringing water glasses to put by a sink, and I immediately registered, "Pay attention: this person is special." Twenty years later, it gives me great pleasure to recall the deep-body knowing of that moment.

I believe everyone has such an inner "guidance system". Scientific breakthroughs, brilliance in business, and successful partnerships often track back to moments of clarity that individuals were courageous enough to act on.

Smaller details of life can also benefit from intuition, such as the best route to take on a holiday weekend, which networking leads to follow, or a good gift for someone you barely know.

Despite the grace and ease intuition offers, it is common for people to ignore its insights, or to feel the messages cannot be trusted. We have been schooled to favour rational, logical thought, and few institutions accept anything else.

At the same time, while not yet mainstream in Western culture, there is now far greater openness to cultivating our latent capacities for intuitive knowing.

But how?

Assume that you are already intuitive, and that your task is to pay more attention to intuitive insights and hunches at the edges of your awareness. Notice how intuition differs from when your thoughts are coming from fear, confusion, or a busy monkey-mind.

Then try the Coin Toss tool, a practice I have adapted from a powerful personal development tool called the Game of Transformation[5]. Here is how to do it.

Other indicators

Other clues that my intuition is accurate are:

- a glowing sensation in the middle of my chest;
- a tingling sensation in the palms of my hands;
- a subtler sense that I call "alignment", where it feels as if all the vertebrae and molecules in my body are lined up and working in support of the same purpose;
- I am generally calm, detached, and at peace.

---

5 For more information see Game of Transformation in Further Resources on page 90.

COIN TOSS

1. Start by opening to the possibility that you can have easy access to your intuitive knowing. Others have done this. So can you!

2. Set an intention to strengthen your intuitive "muscle".

3. Clarify your purpose for doing inner work.

4. Center and ground. For more on this see Groundwork on page 19.

5. Dedicate the inner work and ask in your own way that it serve the highest.

6. Become receptive (see Becoming Receptive sidebar on page 29), and welcome insights from your intuitive knowing about the question or issue.

7. Listen for your intuition. You will often receive an immediate hit. Sometimes people turn away from these initial responses because they do not fit with what they expected,

Getting ready for Coin Toss

- Pick a coin with a size and weight that works for you. I use a quarter.

- Decide whether you will catch the coin or let it fall on the ground.

- Practice flipping your coin, making sure that it flips at least three times in the air. Ask someone to show you how if you have not learned this particular life skill.

- Decide which side of the coin confirms your intuition – heads or tails. You could say when the coin lands heads up, that means "Yes" or accurate intuition while tails indicates "No" or faulty intuition. The other way is fine too. What matters is that you define the terms.

what they want, or what they feel is acceptable. When intuition tests "faulty", people generally can track back to discounting their initial hit.

8. Frame your intuitive hit as a statement about what is true in this moment: "My intuitive hit is _____."

    o   Do not frame things as a question (for example: "Does it serves the highest for me to go to the meeting?"), but as your intuitive answer to the question ("It serves the highest for me to go to the meeting.").

    o   Do not proceed unless you are using a present-time statement, (see inset page 43).

9. Prepare to flip a coin – see sidebar on page 49. Always place the coin with the "Yes" side up as it rests in the "launch" position.

10. Flip the coin immediately after saying or holding in mind the present-time statement that expresses your intuition.

    o   If you intended to catch the coin, but drop it, repeat steps 9-10.

11. Act on what you get.

Skeptical?

How can this process be a valid way to check intuition?

If the science of probability says an evenly-weighted coin has a 50-50 chance of landing heads up, then how can tossing a coin verify intuition? Or is it possible that we have a subconscious ability to control how many times the coin flips and therefore how it lands? (This is the rationale for ensuring the coin flips at least three times.)

Try it, and see what happens! You might try experimenting with simple things where stakes are low, paying attention to how they turn out in the end.

For a conceptual framework, I recommend Carl Jung's wonderful Foreword to Richard Wilhelm's translation of *The I Ching*. People seeking guidance from this ancient Chinese text use coin toss to determine the best response. Jung sees meaningful "synchronicity" in what most Westerners regard as random coin-tossing probabilities. He also challenges reproducibility as the definition of scientific validity.

> *"This assumption [of how the I Ching works]
> involves a certain curious principle that I have termed
> synchronicity, a concept that formulates a point of
> view diametrically opposed to that of causality. Since
> the latter is merely statistical truth and not absolute,
> it is a sort of working hypothesis of how events evolve
> one out of another, whereas synchronicity takes the
> coincidence of events in space and time as meaning
> something more than mere chance, namely a peculiar
> interdependence of objective events among themselves
> as well as with the subjective (psychic) states of the
> observer or observers."*[6]

In other words, there is synchronicity between the questioner's mind and how coins land when using *The I Ching*.

It works.

Then again, there is a chance that it works for people who believe it works, or are open to it working, belief being part of our subjective state.

If you are a doubter, then leave aside the process of checking intuition by tossing coins, and keep the part about cultivating intuition – note your intuitive hits and see if they

---

6 See Wilhelm, *The I Ching*, page xxiv.

are later validated by how things turn out. The real goal, after all, is to access and trust your intuitive knowing.

Finer points

- While I can have accurate intuition without the buzzing sensations described earlier, I am always spot on when I feel the buzz.

- With years of practice, I am one of the best coin flippers I know, launching coins into high, tight arcs that spin rapidly, and fall cleanly into my waiting hand. Sometimes, though, it feels as though the coin is "thick". I set the coin on my thumb and fingers as normal, but when I flick, the coin rises only inches, without spinning, and flops into my hand or (not infrequently) onto the floor. Other times, I cannot catch the coin because the flipping arc carries it too far away. I used to stubbornly persist, repeating the process until I had a clean toss, flipping three times and landing in my hand. Invariably the coins came up "tails" – faulty intuition. Now I short circuit the process, and read a thick or errant coin as a "No", often sensing that the deeper feedback is, *"Don't even ask."*

Possible pitfalls

- Some people misunderstand this tool, seeing it as no different than the common practice of letting chance decide things by flipping a coin. The Coin Toss tool is actually more about strengthening your intuition than making decisions: used properly, coin toss gives instant and accurate feedback as to the truth or falsity of thoughts you hold in mind. Proper use of coin toss includes setting the intention to check an intuition, and opening to trust the process.

t as framed.
be wary of
ng to con-
intuition
ays noth-
r).

; to be in control and know
al to try to frame statements
em is that intuition is always
nt. Coin Toss is meaningless for
e. I repeat: Coin Toss is meaning-
the future.

k and easy way to check intuition
ound myself checking in when I do
cultivating my intuition, I am using

able of
anding
ed my
es and

right
ly to
ode"

an
ive
ur
u

usions

ind a gift for a friend, and I had the
something by a favourite potter. I
test the statement: "Sue likes John's style
I got a "Yes".

to John's studio when I realized I had
onclusion that pottery would be a great gift
attached to my idea, I tuned in about the
'A piece of John's pottery would be an
ift for Sue", and flipped the coin again. This
a "No".

the pottery idea, I tuned in about what would
at gift. My intuition suggested sending funds for
orm of body work. "Yes!", said the coin.

a card with a cheque, Sue chose yoga classes, and
nce told me of the ongoing benefits and joy the gift
given her. When I told her about the pottery idea,
said that while she likes beautiful pottery, the cheque
body work had been a much better gift.

- Coin Toss will respond precisely to the statemen
  No more, and no less. This means we need to
  assumptions, unjustified inferences, and jumpi
  clusions. It is very easy to misrepresent what you
  is telling you. That your intuition confirms ABC s
  ing about DEF (see Jumping to conclusions sideb

Learning new tricks

For my first four years as a yoga student, I was incap
spreading my toes, an important foundation for all st
poses. I trusted it was possible, as I routinely watch
instructor create enormous openings between her big to
the next in line.

Then one day, I "found" the muscle that moved my
big toe to the left. Even then, it did not translate quick
the other foot. It took me about 10 minutes to learn the "c
for getting my body to do this simple thing.

I believe we have wonderful latent capacities we
cultivate if we so choose, and top tier among these is intuit
knowing. I hope you will put time into awakening yo
intuition. It will save you time in the long run, and help y
live a life full of joy, flow, and alignment with purpose.

6
Guiding Images

Several years ago, I began tuning in for a guiding image at the beginning of each new project. Having a guiding image is a quick and potent way to orient myself when starting out, and a helpful touchstone at later decision points.

A guiding image is a symbol or picture that comes from our inner world. Because the image comes from within, it is "worth a thousand words", often encoding deep meaning and insight in a single flash.

An example comes from my work on a food security project in the beautiful Sea to Sky Corridor north of Vancouver. Many children go hungry there, and a regional planning group of early childhood service providers wanted to do something about it.

As part of developing a proposal, I sat in meditation for five minutes. After laying the groundwork and calling to mind what I knew about the region, I asked for a guiding image. What came was a picture of a huge cauldron simmering in the middle of a village square.

I recognized one of my favourite folktales:

The Stone Soup Story

Three hungry soldiers come to a village and go door to door asking for food. The villagers are poor and, unwilling to feed the soldiers, they hide their food. Then the soldiers put a huge cauldron of water on a fire in the middle of the village square. Curious villagers come to find out what is happening. The soldiers say they are making Stone Soup, and add three stones to the pot. To the skeptics, they say the soup would taste much better with a bit of pepper, then with a bit of cabbage, then with a bit of potato, and so on. In the end, the whole village feasts on soup everyone has happily made some small contribution to.

Inspired by the image, I started by listening for what "cauldron" I might place in the middle of the metaphorical village square. Through conversations, I soon found an idea that resonated with key informants: a series of workshops about growing food and food-related businesses.

The topic and keynote speaker drew people with a passion for food, and by following up with those people, I began linking and amplifying their efforts, thanks to modest seed funding.

Throughout what became a successful project, I was guided by the kernel in the Stone Soup story: everything needed is already in the community, and people want to help when they can be part of a community happening. I have received similar support and clarity through using guiding images in many other personal and professional circumstances.

- Given our very human desire to be in control and know what will happen, it is normal to try to frame statements about the future. The problem is that intuition is always and only about this moment. Coin Toss is meaningless for statements about the future. I repeat: Coin Toss is meaningless for statements about the future.

- Coin Toss is such a quick and easy way to check intuition that I have sometimes found myself checking in when I do not need to. Instead of cultivating my intuition, I am using Coin Toss as a crutch.

Jumping to conclusions

Once I wanted to find a gift for a friend, and I had the idea of giving her something by a favourite potter. I flipped a coin to test the statement: "Sue likes John's style of pottery", and got a "Yes".

I was about go to John's studio when I realized I had leapt to the conclusion that pottery would be a great gift for Sue. Still attached to my idea, I tuned in about the statement: "A piece of John's pottery would be an excellent gift for Sue", and flipped the coin again. This time I got a "No".

Dropping the pottery idea, I tuned in about what would be a great gift. My intuition suggested sending funds for some form of body work. "Yes!", said the coin.

I sent a card with a cheque, Sue chose yoga classes, and has since told me of the ongoing benefits and joy the gift has given her. When I told her about the pottery idea, she said that while she likes beautiful pottery, the cheque for body work had been a much better gift.

- Coin Toss will respond precisely to the statement as framed. No more, and no less. This means we need to be wary of assumptions, unjustified inferences, and jumping to conclusions. It is very easy to misrepresent what your intuition is telling you. That your intuition confirms ABC says nothing about DEF (see Jumping to conclusions sidebar).

Learning new tricks

For my first four years as a yoga student, I was incapable of spreading my toes, an important foundation for all standing poses. I trusted it was possible, as I routinely watched my instructor create enormous openings between her big toes and the next in line.

Then one day, I "found" the muscle that moved my right big toe to the left. Even then, it did not translate quickly to the other foot. It took me about 10 minutes to learn the "code" for getting my body to do this simple thing.

I believe we have wonderful latent capacities we can cultivate if we so choose, and top tier among these is intuitive knowing. I hope you will put time into awakening your intuition. It will save you time in the long run, and help you live a life full of joy, flow, and alignment with purpose.

6
Guiding Images

Several years ago, I began tuning in for a guiding image at the beginning of each new project. Having a guiding image is a quick and potent way to orient myself when starting out, and a helpful touchstone at later decision points.

A guiding image is a symbol or picture that comes from our inner world. Because the image comes from within, it is "worth a thousand words", often encoding deep meaning and insight in a single flash.

An example comes from my work on a food security project in the beautiful Sea to Sky Corridor north of Vancouver. Many children go hungry there, and a regional planning group of early childhood service providers wanted to do something about it.

As part of developing a proposal, I sat in meditation for five minutes. After laying the groundwork and calling to mind what I knew about the region, I asked for a guiding image. What came was a picture of a huge cauldron simmering in the middle of a village square.

I recognized one of my favourite folktales:

The Stone Soup Story

Three hungry soldiers come to a village and go door to door asking for food. The villagers are poor and, unwilling to feed the soldiers, they hide their food. Then the soldiers put a huge cauldron of water on a fire in the middle of the village square. Curious villagers come to find out what is happening. The soldiers say they are making Stone Soup, and add three stones to the pot. To the skeptics, they say the soup would taste much better with a bit of pepper, then with a bit of cabbage, then with a bit of potato, and so on. In the end, the whole village feasts on soup everyone has happily made some small contribution to.

Inspired by the image, I started by listening for what "cauldron" I might place in the middle of the metaphorical village square. Through conversations, I soon found an idea that resonated with key informants: a series of workshops about growing food and food-related businesses.

The topic and keynote speaker drew people with a passion for food, and by following up with those people, I began linking and amplifying their efforts, thanks to modest seed funding.

Throughout what became a successful project, I was guided by the kernel in the Stone Soup story: everything needed is already in the community, and people want to help when they can be part of a community happening. I have received similar support and clarity through using guiding images in many other personal and professional circumstances.

Using guiding images

Guiding images can offer insights in countless situations. To name a few, guiding images provide an entry point to our inner knowing about the following sorts of questions:

- How best to frame a project or task
- How to understand a relationship
- What to bring to a situation
- What to leave behind
- What is seeking to unfold
- What is in your way
- What you most need to be aware of
- What dynamic is at play in a situation
- What is a key next step
- How to simplify things
- And many other situations

For me, the challenge is not how to use the tool. It is *remembering* to use the tool! Here is how you can access your own guiding images.

GUIDING IMAGE

1. Clarify your purpose for doing inner work. If helpful, use one of the focus statements listed above.

2. Find a place to sit quietly in meditation.

3. Center and ground. For more on this see Groundwork, page 19.

4. Dedicate the inner work, and ask in your own way that it serve the highest.

5. When you feel ready, bring to mind your focus/question and ask for an image to guide you.

6. Trust what comes. Do not be surprised if it is not visual.

You might get your insights through body sensations, or, like a colleague of mine, they might be auditory – her insights come predominantly through popular songs, of which she knows thousands!

7. Take time to be with the image, and invite it to share the insights it brings.

8. If the image is confusing, ask for another image to help you understand it, or get help from other inner work tools such as Automatic Writing or Coin Toss.

Finer points

- Guiding images are dense with meaning, and because they come from within, they are custom tailored to each of us.

Working with two images

It can be powerful to have two guiding images, one that expresses the current situation and another that captures a future ideal.

This exercise was extremely helpful in the beginning stages of writing this book. In the first image, I saw myself as a little girl lost in the woods. The image captured the dynamic at play when I was blocked and unable to write.

In the second I was a crone: I was beyond being concerned about what others think about me and free to speak my truth.

Many times when I was swirling in fear or frozen in self doubt, I recognized that Lost Little Girl was in play, and chose Crone instead. The shift in my body was instantaneous. It was as if a different operating system slipped in, and the writing flowed.

For example, the Stone Soup folktale is one of my favourites, so for me the image of the steaming cauldron in the middle of the village square was both inspiring and full of clarity.

- Guiding images are similar to dreams: sometimes the meaning is obvious, and sometimes we need to dig a little to get the message.

- When reflecting on the meaning of an image, I find there is a textural difference between when I have an authentic intuitive insight, and when I am jumping quickly to an interpretation that I am comfortable with. When I am jumping to conclusions, it feels like I am grabbing – quick and tight-fisted – as though I close my mind as soon as I have latched onto an interpretation that keeps me comfortable. The texture of an accurate intuition is open – like an offering that sits in an open hand – with lots of space and light around it, happy for me to take it or leave it.

Possible pitfalls

- The more attached, disturbed, or agitated I am, the more likely I am to interpret an image in a way that brings me relief, and in a way that says what I want to hear. When I do this, the power of an image can amplify my denial and delusion. If you are like me, the greatest risk with guiding images is to be more guided by your ego than the actual image, as images can be twisted to mean just about anything.

- Being mindful of this potential pitfall is a big part of undoing its power. Because I am aware of the risk, I am vigilant, and often ask myself if I am truly open to what an image is trying to tell me. I find it is helpful to slow down the process, take time to look again at an image, and choose to trust that what it reveals is a gift – even if I do not like what I see.

- It can also be helpful to discern whether I am too agitated to use this form of inner work. Automatic Writing or Burning Your Wood might be more appropriate tools.

Interpreting an image

Recently, an old friend came to town. She is someone I have worked and played with, laughed, and had delicious conversations with, long into many nights.

It had been almost twenty years since we had any regular contact. For whatever reason it felt like we could not talk two sentences on any subject without creating a competitive dynamic that was irksome.

I was triggered (perhaps most triggered) when she said that my reactions were all my stuff. I felt so poked and piqued that a big part of me wanted to run away. Yet another part knew there was a huge gift for me – if I had the courage to face my insecurities.

Seeking guidance, I tuned in for an image to support my next steps in the friendship. I saw a heart, and interpreted this as being a *symbol of love*. I jumped to the conclusion that this meant glossing over the conflict, and reaching out in love and friendship (no need to go into the uncomfortable swamp...).

I could feel, though, a telltale "grabbing" energy. So I slowed down to receive the image more fully: the heart was a dull grey. It was made of plastic and coated in fake-velvet. This time I took the image to mean: *a once vital friendship is now grey – more form than substance; I should let the friendship go.* Knowing I was agitated, and had been jumping to comforting conclusions, I used muscle testing to check the accuracy of this latest interpretation. "No".

Tuning in to my intuition, I posited: *the image means I need to shed outer form to uncover the core connection of love that is always there.* This time I got a "Yes" – further corroborated by a tingling feeling in my chest and arms and at the crown of my head.

My personality said, "*Drat.*" Part of me wanted out, but my deeper truth was a complete trust in the wisdom of the fuzzy grey heart, and a commitment to the insights it was bringing me. As a result of this process, I renewed my commitment to the friendship, and to facing the issues my friend brings up for me.

Try it!

Guiding images work. A picture is worth a thousand words and, when a project is at a crossroads or you are stumped about what to do next, a guiding image is easy to remember and draw inspiration from.

7
Inner Guides

I have two inner guides who have been lightening my load since the early 90s. Georgina is from the deep South. She wears floral print dresses stretched over her ample hips and bosom, and laughs from deep in her belly. She is a wise and big-hearted grandma, and to be hugged by Georgina is to feel loved and consoled, no matter how bad things seem.

Jason is stillness and peace personified in a beautiful, long-haired young man. He is fierce, fearless, and free; a radiant and quiet being with clear brown eyes. When he looks at me I feel seen.

I connect with Georgina and Jason by taking myself – through a guided visualization – to a small log cabin in the woods. The interior is dark and rough-hewn. Georgina is always on the left, and I generally visit with her first. Jason waits patiently in the shadows to the right, ready to complement and deepen the energy and insights I get from Georgina.

As I understand it, my guides are not external, independent

beings, but rather key parts of myself projected into two characters. By opening an inner space to meet with them, I can dialogue with higher aspects of myself.

I first met these guides through the following guided visualization. I use the same exercise any time I want to reconnect with them.

Your guides will be different, reflecting the uniqueness of you and your inner symbology. Yours might not be human, but instead animals, energies, or other beings. You might find a different guide each time, or many guides. Be open to what comes.

Here is how to do it.

INNER GUIDES

1. Clarify your question or purpose for doing inner work. For suggestions, see the list on page 57.

2. Find a place to sit quietly in meditation.

3. Center, ground, and dedicate your inner work to serving the highest. For more on this see Groundwork, page 19.

4. Close your eyes. Visualize yourself in a beautiful meadow in the height of summer. Take a few moments to see what is at your feet, to hear the sounds, to feel the air, to notice the smells.

5. Once you have a sense of being in the meadow, look around until you see a path leading to a nearby forest. Follow the path out of the meadow, noticing your surroundings as you go. Once in the forest, keep on the path until it leads you to a building.

6. Take a moment to see the building and to find the entrance. When you are ready, go inside. Be open to the possibility of meeting a guide.

7. Once inside, notice your surroundings and how it feels to be there. Look around for your guide.

8. Greet your guide. It can be helpful to ask for his/her/its name, and to make eye contact.

9. Have a conversation. Bring forward your focus or question.

10. At some point, the conversation will naturally wane. It can be helpful to ask, *"Is there anything else you want to add?"*

11. Thank your inner guide for the insights.

12. Optional: look around to see if there is another inner guide in the space. If so, have a conversation with this new guide.

13. When you want to leave, say thank you and good-bye to your guide(s).

14. Look around the inner space once more. Take a moment to consciously cross the threshold as you leave the building. Return the way you came: take the same path through the forest, back to the meadow, and notice more about the forest as you go. Once back in the meadow, again see, hear, feel, and smell what is there.

15. Take several deep breaths. When you are ready, open your eyes and bring yourself back into the room.

Finer points

- Before beginning, ask yourself if you are truly open to this way of working. Basic trust in the process needs to be there, or you are better off working with other tools.

- There is no need to limit yourself to two guides, or to the guided visualization described above. You can use different visualizations, and link with many different guides and wise beings.

- When you frame your focus or deepen a conversation with your inner guide, open-ended questions are a powerful way to gain insights. Examples include:

  o   What is going on? What is the dynamic at play?
  o   What am I not noticing that is important?
  o   Is there anything else I should be aware of?
  o   Is there anything you would like to add?

  If I have come to my inner guides with a specific burning issue, I generally include one or two open-ended questions at the end of the conversation. Often their answers take my understanding to a significantly deeper level – typically more heart and less head.

- Some people are uncomfortable with closing their eyes for this exercise. If you are one of them, try the visualization with your eyes open. You might also try it before going to sleep or on waking. Both are times when we tend to be more open to inner wisdom.

Possible pitfalls

I have not experienced any pitfalls with this way of working. If you encounter any, please let me know.

Always there

I always feel a kind of homecoming when I connect with my inner guides, and deep gratitude for this inner source of wisdom and support. Whether I use this tool often or only occasionally, just knowing my guides are there gives me strength. In case it is the same for you, I hope you will try this tool at least once.

8
Framing

What if we can shift in a heartbeat from limitation to freedom?

What if a simple change in perspective changes everything?

Framing and reframing are about consciously choosing what we focus on, and therefore how we see life and all its situations. Framing calls us to be more aware of what is normally marginalized or on the periphery of our awareness. Framing invites us to see our situation from multiple perspectives, and then to choose the frames that are the most alive and life-giving.

One of my favourite examples is the choice between deficit-based and asset-based approaches to working in communities. Our cultural bias is to focus on deficits, seeing life as a problem that needs fixing. In this frame, I could see a person, for example, as paraplegic, unemployed, and depressed. Choosing to see strengths, I can see the same person as a highly-skilled woodworker, a brilliant musician, and a patient teacher. Then instead of working against huge odds, I am working with possibility. Instead of a limiting helper-helpee relationship, we can be creative people supporting each other to do what we love.

Changing the frame can radically alter how we perceive and engage in a situation, both inside (our thoughts and feelings) and out (our actions and effectiveness).

Closer to home, I recently reframed my life from a series of thresholds – points of drama, hesitation, and confusion – to a continuum of grace and flow. For many years I had a habit of saying to myself, *"I have never done this before,"* code for *"I am scared and want to run away"*. Now when I catch myself hesitating about any next step, I take a few big breaths and let go into the flow. I am literally changing the story I tell myself about myself.

When I am ready to make a change (and I find it becomes easier and easier with practice), this is what I do.

REFRAMING

1. The starting point is recognizing that something is amiss – you are feeling out of sorts or somehow not aligned.

2. Notice what the "story" is. How would you describe your situation to a good friend?

3. Open up to seeing the situation in a different way, one that serves the highest.

    This is a form of setting intention. Since our perspective shapes how we feel and act, opening to seeing things a different way is the same as opening to change.

4. Be open to what comes.

    For me, a new way of seeing often comes as an intuition. When I open up to see things differently, I loosen my attachment to the current story. The new perspective often comes in a flash, as though it had been waiting in the wings, so hoping I would let it in. Other times, insights come from outside, and arrive through a conversation or a snippet on the radio.

5. If the new way to frame things resonates, choose to embrace it. And keep re-choosing it if the old story reasserts itself.

6. Repeat steps 1-5 whenever things feel blocked, constricted, or out of alignment.

Finer points

- Willingness to use this tool is half the process. Reframing requires us to open up to the possibility of things being different and better. I think of it as breaking the thrall of current reality.

- Reframing can amplify the effectiveness of every other inner work tool. This is because it matters how we frame things when we clarify the focus of our inner work. Do we ask, for example, about priorities from a limited menu of options, or do we invite options from a bigger or infinite menu?

- We have the choice in each moment to see the glass as half empty, half full, overflowing, or any number of ways. A powerful shortcut in framing or reframing is to cultivate gratitude for what is. No matter how dark things get, make a practice of finding even one small thing to be grateful for. Being grateful supports living a life of joy.

- Perhaps the most potent form of reframing is to choose how we see ourselves. Do we frame our self image primarily at the personality level (with gender, preferences, and world-views) or also include a deeper, "soul" level? Do we see and experience ourselves as separate, or as one with all that is?

Potential pitfalls

- Reframing, and reframing the reframe, can lead to a kind of "it doesn't matter" relativism where you open to so many ways of seeing a situation that you become lost or paralyzed. Then instead of accessing clarity and inner knowing, we are swirling in monkey-mind. When this happens, I find the best thing is to stop and do groundwork until I am again oriented to serving the highest. If I am too caught in doubt or confusion to do so, then I first do something that shifts my energy, like going for a brisk walk, dancing, or having a shower.

- Due to the strength of our egos, there is always a risk of using reframing as a way of avoiding what is disturbing and staying where things are comfortable. Ask yourself if you are avoiding anything as you reframe situations. It is generally better to deal with conflicts and disturbances directly, rather than leaving them to fester or drain energy.

Swimming completely free

The stories we tell ourselves are like life rafts: we cling to them as if our lives depend on them. If we outgrow one and decide to move on, then we generally latch onto another story/life raft as soon as we can. My husband has a deep aspiration to let go of all life rafts and swim free, without clinging to any story. This is one way to express the yearning many of us feel to be fully authentic. I think we get there gradually, by getting comfortable with letting go of one story after another.

9
Burning Your Wood

There is a woman in my life who gets my goat. Her voice is like fingernails on a chalk board; she sees the negative side of situations, and complains all the time. I feel bludgeoned in her presence, like a daisy meeting a steamroller.

When I find myself going out of my way to avoid her, I know I am not free. Part of me is caught, embroiled in circumstances.

"The way out is through," I tell myself. Instead of running away from her, I need to sit in the fire, being curious and acknowledging my half of the situation.

Burning Your Wood is an inner work tool for dealing with challenging people and situations. It involves identifying what triggers us, and reflecting on whether the triggers are something we do or need to be doing. The final step is to act on the insights, so that the "wood" (the part of us that got triggered) gets all burned up, and there is none of it left to catch fire.

Here is how to do it.

BURNING YOUR WOOD

1. Notice that you are triggered. It could be by a person, a circumstance, a new idea.

2. Bring warm, curious attention to your triggered self. Assume both that your behaviour makes sense, and that there are wondrous possibilities for greater freedom. Instead of judging yourself, be curious about the pretzel you have contorted yourself into.

3. Ask your inner knowing what it is that triggers you. Trust what comes. You can use Automatic Writing, Guiding Image, and other tools, if helpful.

4. [Optional] Ask: *"Is there anything else?"* Often, we quickly name the things that are relatively easy for us to acknowledge, but deeper triggers need a bit more probing.

5. Appreciate yourself for looking at what triggers you. Simply being aware will start to change things.

6. Reflect on whether what triggers you is something you also do, or something you need to do more. The trigger indicates the quality or characteristic where you are not in alignment. If you are triggered by someone you see as "bossy" it could mean that you, too, are bossy, and/or it could mean you need to be bossier!

7. Act on the insights. The wood is only truly burned when we take the new insights into new behaviour.

Here is what I gleaned from burning my wood relating to the steamroller woman:

- Be more forthright in expressing my feelings and thoughts
- Acknowledge when I am needy and want more attention
- Notice and stop myself when I, too, am like a steamroller

The benefits are both that I live a richer life, and that I am less irritated by the troublesome people and situations in my life. Often, the results feel miraculous: I burn my wood and I find myself *liking* a previously challenging person or circumstance.

Finer points

- One of the simplest ways I notice my triggers is to listen to myself talking to other people. If I am complaining or judging, it means that I am triggered. Another is to catch myself saying, *"Always"*, *"Never"*, *"Everything"*, *"Every time"*. Such black and white thinking is a sure sign of being off-center.

- Burning our wood can feel like a full time job. Most of us are triggered multiple times per hour. Fortunately, we do not have to do it all. Burning our wood about one issue ripples out, freeing us to some degree in all similar circumstances.

- I generally burn my wood when issues come up in significant relationships and whenever I am particularly upset. If it feels like the stakes are too high, burn your wood about smaller triggers (for example, about the person who cut in front of you at the grocery store, rather than your demanding family member).

- See whether you notice a connection between small triggers and big ones.

- Notice that you do not need to speak to the other person to burn your wood. It is not about changing them. It is about changing your perspective. They are a mirror that helps you see yourself. Repeated applications of this practice helps one realize that *"there is no out there out there"*. Everything we see is a reflection of what is going on inside.

"But that takes the fun out of it... I can't complain righteously anymore!" I have felt this SO often – a kind of downer. But just as often as I have burned my wood, I have gained something infinitely more precious: a delicious freedom, spaciousness, and peace.

- One can burn wood about people we admire too, or people we find intimidating. This is the important other half of the picture: the times triggers spring from potential within us that is seeking to unfold. Burning my wood about spiritual teachers I admire has been particularly powerful.

- Burning my wood does not mean I never do the work of changing outer circumstances. In fact, by prefacing outer work with this form of inner work, I am more effective in my actions since I am able to speak and act from a non-triggered place.

- There is a difference between being triggered and making a discerning observation. When we judge, our hearts are closed, and there is agitation in mind and body. In discernment, we are aware of what IS without closing our hearts, and we have clarity and peace in the body-mind.

Possible pitfalls

- This form of inner work can be turned on its head. Instead of bringing greater insight, personal responsibility and informed action, it can block all three.

- Typically, this happens when we do inner work to relieve agitation, but stop before we engage in aware and centered action. The goal of inner work should be the alignment of all aspects of our lives with what is most authentic and true. Backing away from where our inner wisdom takes us is not only a form of self-betrayal, but can cut us off from our inner knowing.

Even easier

Recently I was in a workshop. Mid-afternoon, someone complained about the heat and another person turned on noisy ceiling fans. I was instantly triggered. I hate noisy fans. I have a well-developed identity as a noisy fan hater. "I" would rather suffocate from oppressive muggy heat than turn on a fan.

So there I was, working up a lovely head of steam when, *poof,* I shifted perspective. The fan was no longer an issue.

I was delighted. Really? Not an issue?

"Really." More real than the old story.

And delicious. Like the wind-in-the-hair freedom of coasting on a bicycle.

I went from tight and contracted to open and free.

And there was no processing.

It was simply shifting perspective from self to Self, from personality to bare awareness.

The deepest inner work is really about shifting perspective: the possibility, in this instant, to be completely at peace, at ease, in joy – no matter what is going on.

No work.

No burning wood.

No surrender.

Nothing that happens in time.

Just *poof* a different perspective.

10
Multiple Options

The Multiple Options tool is a quick way to make decisions and discern priorities. It involves brainstorming ideas or potential directions, and then a simple process for sorting and ranking them using Muscle Testing, Coin Toss, or another inner work tool.

I suggested this approach to a friend who felt stuck, and unable to leave a toxic workplace, even though she said, "Every part of my body knows it is wrong for me."

Part of my friend's stuckness came from staying too long in a bad situation. As with any dysfunctional relationship, staying can lead to diminished self-confidence and feeling that we have no options. But another part of her stuckness came from being at a loss about what to do next.

How many of us are putting in time in a way that is quietly killing us?

How many of us are bewildered by choice to the point where we stay stuck?

In 2003, I knew it was time to leave a fundraising consultancy where I had worked for two and a half years. What finally called the question was an out-of-nowhere pain in my right foot. The message? Time for me to *"put my right foot forward"* – almost too cute for words.

The next day I told my employer I was giving notice that I would be giving notice soon, and I was gone within three months.

"What next?"

I had no shortage of ideas. Rather I had so many that I was paralyzed with indecision. Should I put my energy into getting a job or studying, into writing, or into actualizing this, that, or the other dream?

Enter Dekyi Lee, a retired Buddhist nun who had been a mentor and friend in Scotland. I had not seen her for seven years; the timing felt uncanny.

She told me about a tool she uses in such circumstances: *"When I need to choose what is next at a time of transition, I brainstorm everything I can think of, and then do a visualization to sort them into "Yes's" and "No's"."*

That was just the logjam-breaking suggestion I needed, and one I have since used hundreds of times for everything from big transition decisions to creating a dinner party invite list.

Here is how to do it.

MULTIPLE OPTIONS

1. Create a time and space with privacy and no interruptions.

2. Frame your purpose (for example, to gain insight into what to do next). If relevant, clarify the timeframe you are working with (today, this week, this year).

3. Confirm that it is appropriate to use inner work for this purpose. I tune into my intuition. You could also use Coin Toss, Guiding Image or Automatic Writing.

4. Brainstorm lots of options and write them down. Mind mapping can be helpful for this (see Buzan in Further Resources).

5. Invite yourself to come up with even more options, the ones on the periphery hoping to be noticed.

6. Always include "Other" at least once, in case there is a priority you have missed.

7. Using index cards (or other cards identical in size, colour, and shape) create one card for each option: number each of the options you have brainstormed on your list or mind map, and then write corresponding numbers on the cards. This is both quicker (writing "2" versus "Research") and more environmentally friendly: you can use the same cards over and over.

8. Turn the cards face down, shuffle them well, and put them in a pile close at hand.

9. Ground yourself (see Groundwork, page 19), reconnect with your specific intention, and ask that your inner work serve the highest.

10. In preparation for sorting the cards, decide where you will create a "Yes" pile and where you create a "No" pile (for example, to your right or your left).

11. Choose and use an approach to sorting. Options include:

    o Muscle Testing (see page 39). Pick one card and keep it face down. For this specific card, muscle test a statement something like, "This option is a priority." If this muscle tests true, put the card in the "Yes" pile. If it tests false, put the card in the "No" pile. Repeat for each of the cards.

o   Coin Toss (see page 47). Pick one card and keep it face down. While holding this specific card, tune in about whether the card represents a priority option, and frame a present-time statement accordingly. Then put the card down and use Coin Toss to check the accuracy of your statement. Put the card in the appropriate "Yes" or "No" pile. For example, if you intuit the option is a priority, and this is confirmed by Coin Toss, put the card in the "Yes" pile. Repeat for each of the cards.

o   Blind Pick. Start by deciding how many cards you will pick. I tend to limit the number of priorities to five or fewer. Arrange the cards facedown and spread out so each card is separate from the others. Connect with your intention, and then pick the number of cards you decided to pick.

12. Act on what you get.

When I suggested this exercise to the friend who felt stuck in a toxic work place, she looked both intrigued and apprehensive.

If using this exercise at a time of major transition does not feel comfortable, try it for lower-stake decisions. For example, I often use this tool for allocating time among competing priorities for a single day, and to clarify which research leads to follow up on.

If it works for you as it does for me, the "Yes" answers you get will ring true.

Finer points

- It is helpful if the cards are identical when face down, so you are not influenced by knowing which is which. If a card gets marked or dog-eared in a way that stands out, replace it.

- It requires trust not to second-guess the process if you get a long streak of "Yes's" or "No's". Initially I was disconcerted when this would happen. "It should be a "Yes" next after all those "No's". With practice, I have come to completely trust the accuracy of this way of discerning between options.

- Again, to prevent interference from the part of us that likes to be in control, look at the results only after all the cards are sorted. That way you will not be second-guessing which options are left.

- When "Other" comes as one of the priorities, brainstorm further options (steps 4 and 5). Include "Other" as an option in this new round (step 6). Then complete the rest of the process.

An "Other" experience

Once in a busy period, I kept getting "Other", until at last I included "Invoice clients" among the options. Invoicing was something I typically relegated to the bottom of the priority pile. Once I added invoicing, it was the top priority when I blind picked among 15 "Yes" options.

Reflecting on this experience, I realized I had been undervaluing my personal sustainability in favour of the projects I was engaged in. Now I see that invoicing is like breathing: I need to keep doing it to be able to keep working.

- If you get a large pile of "Yes's" and want guidance on where to start, set the intention of clarifying priorities and do a further round of sorting. The approach I typically use is a blind pick (see step 11 above).

- As a further refinement, I often do inner work (usually Coin Toss) about how much time to allocate to a specific task. For instance, it may be a priority to contact my great aunt, but only for a quick call.

- The approaches to picking priorities in step 11 (Muscle Testing, Coin Toss and Blind Pick) are like training wheels to get you to the point of directly accessing your intuition of what is important, and what to do next.

Possible pitfalls

For a brief period, I was like a kid in a candy store, using the Multiple Options exercise on a daily basis. I loved the clarity, and the feeling of being aligned to my highest purpose. I gained experience and developed deep trust in the process, but I was also way out of balance. I was spending almost as much time tuning in about priorities as acting on them. I was not taking personal responsibility for the things I already knew.

From that experience, I have come to believe we should only check our intuition when we are truly uncertain. In my case, there was a natural self-correcting force to the thrall of the "candy store": I got sick of too much candy, and lost my connection to flow, synchronicity, and joy.

It is from reflecting on the "candy store" experience that I added the third step about tuning in to check the appropriateness of using this tool for a particular purpose.

All this to say, be mindful of potential pitfalls such as a longing to give over responsibility, and not honouring what you already know.

What To Do Monday Morning

In the past, my use of inner work ebbed and flowed. I would go months without using some of the tools in this book. It was as if I just wanted to be a personality banging around and fumbling my way forward. Even though I knew better, I would binge on drama and confusion like someone falling off the wagon, taking a break from sustained positive change.

Early in the creation of this book, I set the intention to make light work in all aspects of the writing, editing, and production. It has worked. Support has come from multiple sources, including free and superb coaching, intuitive and empowering editing, inspired feedback, and practical nuts and bolts suggestions. I have also drawn heavily on inner work tools any time I had a question, or was blocked about next steps.

What I did not anticipate was that writing this book would rewrite me. It is as if I have changed operating systems, upgrading to one that is faster, more fun, and more effective. My life is more aligned with my core purpose, I have stronger access to my authentic voice, and I have a much deeper connection to inner peace and wellbeing.

I also have a much deeper commitment to using inner work on a daily basis.

Really using the tools

I hope you have tried at least one inner work tool by the time you read this, and that you have a sense of the potential benefits for you personally, for your community, and for our world.

The next challenge is to remember to use the tools, and let in all the wonders they offer. How much good news can you stand? How much grace and ease are you willing to receive?

Here is an overview of the many ways I use inner work in a day. I hope it inspires you to experiment with using the tools.

Sketch of a composite day

On waking, and while still lying in bed:

- *Flirts*: Sometimes as I am gently gathering myself for the day, I get clarity about questions and dilemmas, and intuitive "hits" about next steps.

- *Groundwork*: I quickly lay a strong foundation for the day as described on pages 19-25, especially if I have a daunting task before me.

- *Guiding Image*: If the stakes are high, or I just want to give things a boost, I ask for a guiding image for the day.

- *Setting Energy*: My default is to ask for a day filled with joy, peace, ease, and alignment. Some days, I set energy for clarity, honesty, authenticity, and effectiveness (for example, if I am facilitating a complex meeting). I also tune in about what qualities want to come through me in a day or situation, and include them in how I set energy.

Morning routines:

- *Checking Intuition*: I tune in about what to eat for breakfast (and other meals) – asking my body what it needs in terms of food, water, and whether it can tolerate a bit of caffeine.

- *Groundwork*: If the household is chaotic in the morning, I will do "Figure of Eight Breathing" (see pages 24-25) to help me center and thereby support everything to flow more smoothly.

- *Flirts and Guiding Images*: Some mornings, I swim or walk. I often find these two forms of symmetrical physical movement support my openness to intuitive hits, guiding images, and flirts related to whatever is going on in my life.

Work/Play:

- *Groundwork*: I often start by taking a brief moment to check in with myself (as described in Groundwork, see page 19). Am I centered? Am I dedicated to serving the highest? Am I open to what wants to come through?

- *Multiple Options*: When feeling overwhelmed, I use the Multiple Options tool (see page 77) to determine the level of priority and the order for tackling the tasks on my plate. The benefits are profound: I generally experience peace of mind and deep joy to be working on what is most important.

- *Reframing*: Some of my work involves supporting transformative change in organizations and groups. Reframing is a key tool. For example, when clients say things are not working, I ask, *"What IS working?"*, and *"What changes have you made in the past year that you are proud of?"* Framing things appreciatively (seeing the glass as half full) is a simple shift of perception that has profound implications.

- *Coin Toss*: Each day, I make dozens of decisions guided by my intuition. I use Coin Toss to check the accuracy of my intuition about:

  o a sensitive email, proposal or document. For instance, to ensure the content is excellent, the wording is clear, or everything is included;

  o whether to accept a contract, an invitation, or a volunteer opportunity;

  o when to leave one task and pick up another (often my personality wants to quit, but my intuition is to go a bit further);

  o the timing of a phone call, meeting, or even an event;

  o (and whether these examples are enough to convey the point.)

- *Guiding Images*: At the beginning of a new project or initiative, I sit in meditation to get a guiding image. I return to the cushion if I feel stuck or confused about next steps.

- *Setting Energy*: Before important phone calls or meetings, I always set energy as described in Setting the Energy (see page 33).

- *Burning Your Wood*: I aspire to work on myself in a way that mirrors the work I am doing with my clients. For example, if my clients need team-building, better communications, or to shift to a new level, I assume I do too. Working to address my personal issues becomes a significant part of how I serve my clients.

- *Automatic Writing, Burning Your Wood, and Inner Guides*: When I am triggered or caught in fear, conflict or confusion, I use one of these tools to gain insight and shift the dynamic.

At the end of the day:

- *Flirts and Automatic Writing*: Sometimes I reflect on the day, noticing what I have noticed and/or asking to be shown what I have missed that was significant about the day.

Mixing and Matching

Everything knitters create is made from just two types of stitches – knitting and purling. Of course there are lots of variations: two stitches knit together; wool wrapped around more than once; or twisting clumps of stitches to make cables. But that is the point: playing around with a few basic stitches opens many wonderful possibilities.

The same is true with inner work tools. There are many ways one tool can work synergistically with another. Here are three of my favourite pairings:

- Multiple Options with Coin Toss: I use Coin Toss to quickly discern which option to begin with among multiple options I have brainstormed.

- Flirts with Automatic Writing: In response to a specific question or challenge, I "notice what I notice" to identify a flirt, and then do an automatic writing dialogue to access the flirt's insights.

- Guiding Images with Setting the Energy: At the beginning of a consulting project, I do inner work to invite an image to guide my work, and then I set the intention of being guided by that image for the rest of the contract.

These are just three of many possible combinations. I hope you will discover ones that fit for you, and that you find ways to knit inner work into the fabric of each day.

- *Guiding Images*: If I am incomplete or agitated about something that happened in the day, I tune in for a guiding image to gain insights, and to shift whatever needs shifting.

- *Flirts and Intuition*: Sometimes I sleep on decisions, questions, or issues. I put them on the back burner, and then see what comes by morning, either through the thoughts I wake up with, or something that catches my attention.

- *Setting Intention*: I often ask for a great and restorative sleep, and sometimes for dreams to help me with specific challenges.

- *Reframing*: Most evenings, I review the day and express gratitude for things like insights, opportunities, connections, and love. On tough days, I use Reframing to find things to be grateful for in the midst of whatever has been challenging me.

- *Groundwork*: After lights out, I center in big "S" Self (see page 21), answering the question, *"What am I?"* with resting in the awareness of *"I am that"* (which cannot be named). Perhaps this is the most profound inner work of all: to shift how I identify myself from being a someone with a personality, to being one with all that is.

Integrating inner work fully into your life can be like learning to drive a car. At first, there are many things to think about and be aware of, but then, in almost no time, these practices become second nature.

May you make light work of accessing your inner knowing and integrating it into all aspects of your life, and may the highest always be served.

Even Lighter

Here are some quick reminders that distill key points in the book. May they pop into your awareness when you need them.

Stop, and look for an easier way.

Everything you need is inside.

Take a moment to ground and set an intention.

Intend to serve the highest good for all concerned.

Ask: What is my intuition saying?

Ask: Am I in alignment?

Notice what you notice.

The way out is through.

Ask for a guiding image.

Connect with your inner guide(s).

Choose how you frame things.

Burn your wood.

Trust life.

Further Resources

Adyashanti. *The Impact of Awakening*. San Jose, California: Open Gate Publishing, 2000.

Assagioli, Roberto. *Psychosynthesis*. New York, New York: The Viking Press, 1965.

Buzan, Tony. *Mind Map Handbook*. London: Thorsons, 2005.

Caddy, Eileen. *Opening Doors Within*. Findhorn, Scotland: Findhorn Press, 1986.

Diamond, John. *Your Body Doesn't Lie*. New York, New York: Warner Books, 1979.

Doidge, Norman. *The Brain That Changes Itself*. New York, New York: Penguin Books, 2007.

Hawkins, David. *Healing and Recovery*. Sedona, Arizona: Veritas Publishing, 2009.

Jung, Carl. *Synchronicity – An Acausal Connecting Principle*. New York, New York: Routledge and Kegan Paul, 1972.

Katie, Byron. *Loving What Is: Four Questions that Can Change Your Life*. New York, New York: Crown Publishing Group, 2003.

Maclean, Dorothy. *To Hear the Angels Sing*. Issaquah, Washington: Morningtown Press, 1980.

Senge, Peter, and C. Otto Scharmer, Joseph Jaworski, and Betty Sue Flowers. *Presence: Human Purpose and the Field of the Future*. Cambridge, Massachusetts: Society for Organizational Learning, 2004.

Sri Nisargadatta Maharaj. *I Am That.* Durham, NC: The Acorn Press, 1973.

Vaughan, Frances E. *Awakening Intuition.* Garden City, New York: Anchor Press, 1979.

Wilber, Ken. *A Theory of Everything: An integral vision for business, politics, science and spirituality.* Boston, Massachusetts: Shambhala Publications, 2000.

Wilhelm, Richard (translator). *The I Ching.* Princeton, New Jersey: Princeton University Press, 1950.

Other resources

Be The Change Earth Alliance
– www.bethechangeearthalliance.org – An international non-profit organization based in Vancouver, Canada, that supports people to convene and participate in Action Circles for sustained lifestyle change. BTC's programming includes the Make Light Work materials, and can help you can create a support group for integrating inner work tools into your life.

Findhorn Foundation – www.findhorn.org – A spiritual community, ecovillage, and international workshop center that helps to unfold a new human consciousness and create a positive and sustainable future.

The Game of Transformation – www.innerlinks.com – A board game developed at the Findhorn Foundation. Playing the Game deepens awareness of the power of intention (purpose), the potential of intuition, distinctions between intuition and free will, and more.

What's Your Tree – www.whatsyourtree.org – A citizen engagement initiative supporting people to clarify their life purpose and how it can be expressed in service at this time. The program is inspired by Julia Butterfly Hill's 738 day tree sit to save a grove of ancient redwood trees in California.

Acknowledgements

I have been able to make light work in the writing and producing of this book thanks to sharing the journey with many wonderful people. They are Joan Arnott, Tyee Bridge, Heather Briggs (Briggs Strategy), Danny Gillcash, Leslie Hill, Julia Hilton, Barbara Joughin (AAA WordSmith Documentation Services), Susan Hollick-Kenyon, Joanne Kembel, Leslie Kemp, Rik Klingle-Watt, Maureen Jack LaCroix, Tim McCauley, Judi Piggott, Emma Renaerts, Carla Rieger, Irène Scheidegger, Elizabeth Sheehan, Cathryn Wellner, Vanessa Wiebel, Hilary Wilson, and many others. I am particularly grateful to:

- Carole Riddelle, Alan Watson, Deyki Lee Oldershaw, Dianne Falasca, and other members of the Findhorn Foundation, for initiating me in inner work aligned with higher purpose.

- Evan Renaerts, my friend, husband, and collaborator, for believing in me, for carrying more of the load as I was writing, and for brilliant intuitive coaching.

- Saskia Wolsak for companionship, and for developmental editing that helped me find my voice and bring clarity to what once were sticky bits.

- Members of the What's Your Tree National and Regional Leadership Teams for support and inspiration.

- Arnold Mindell, for the concept of *flirts*, and the wisdom in Process Oriented Psychology.

- Ken Wilber, for the way Integral Theory has opened space for more conversation about interior dimensions.

- Jane Sutherland, my mother and associate, for the joy of brainstorming the different phases of the Make Light Work body of work, and for emotional and financial support.

- Derek LaCroix, for breakthrough coaching using the Integral Coaching model, and for suggesting I embrace more grace and ease.

- Bev Kosuljandic, master energy healer, for insights, and for helping me sustainably shift levels.

About the Author

Kate Sutherland uses the tools described in this book on a daily basis in both her personal and professional life. She first became interested in inner work approaches – ways of working based in intuition, intention, perception, and consciousness – when she burned out as a social change activist in the late 1980s. Inner work is the best answer she has found to date in her quest for ways of working that are win-win-win for people, human systems, and the planet.

Kate is a life purpose coach, speaker, workshop leader, and organizational change consultant. In 2010, she created the Make Light Work blog as an online meeting place for sharing inspiration and stories, and to quicken the dissemination of inner work approaches.

Kate specializes in helping people come into better alignment with purpose, both individually and in groups. Her current priority is to make inner work mainstream in North America and around the world – as universal as pencils and cooking pots.

Kate believes that when individuals come into alignment with their core purpose, they help bring human systems into alignment. Kate has deep faith that what is most true within each of us will create a sustainable, just, and fulfilling human presence on this planet.

Kate would love to hear from you! Contribute to the Make Light Work blog at <u>www.katersutherland.com</u> or email Kate at kate@katersutherland.com.

To receive the occasional Make Light Work e-newsletter, to engage Kate for individual coaching or to speak at your conference, or to discuss a project especially designed for your community, company, or organization, please visit www.katersutherland.com or call 1-604-838-1406.

What others say

"Kate Sutherland is a searcher for truths. Whether it is personal truths, community truths or organizational truths, she searches for the highest order of integrity to be found. In these search journeys, Kate uses both sides of her brain, pushing the thinking, the methods and the margins. Kate's work is an example of the kind of integrity one expects of an original: finding the simple truths underlying the complexity and confusion of personal, collective and community change."

Tim Beachy, CEO, United Community Services Co-operative

"Kate has a profound gift for linking personal and social transformational practices. Her ability to articulate ineffable aspects of self-discovery and group process is extraordinary. Kate embodies her purpose and passion in a way that inspires everyone she meets. She brings keen insight and a treasure trove of skills to our grassroots leadership development program."

Jodi Lasseter, National Program Director, What's Your Tree

"Kate understood quickly and intuitively where our group was at and where we wanted to go. Her thoughtful and highly respectful approach helped build the trust we needed in order to get on with the work at hand. With great presence and a deft hand, Kate helped us delve into tough areas of our group culture and dynamic, and move ourselves to a place that was quite different – and better – than where we had been at the beginning of the process. Her recommendations and observations helped the group continue to evolve beyond the day spent with her. Highly recommended!"

Deb Schmitz, Project Coordination and Management,
Nonprofit sector

"Kate Sutherland, along with Evan Renaerts, supported our organization through a difficult transition. Kate's delicate attunement to what needs to arise, combined with her fierce stewardship of the unfolding of truth, helped us to move from a place of hurt and polarity towards a place of healing and maturity. She was unflinching in a large group of passionate individuals, many with strong opinions about what was "right", and rode the balance point between strength and harmlessness in a way that allowed us to let our defenses down and hear each other. We deeply appreciated Kate and Evan's support, which helped us to re-engage with our organization's mission with renewed confidence and integrity."

Elizabeth Neil, Director (2007-2009),
Community Arts Nonprofit

"In 2007, Kate Sutherland organized Our Stories, Demonstrating Change through Storytelling, a conference for Vancouver Coastal Health's SMART Fund. Kate had an amazing knack for bringing together artists, bureaucrats and community developers to orchestrate a conference that honoured the depth and insights of traditional Aboriginal, mainstream and contemporary storytelling. The two day event started on a high note, and just kept getting better. She created an environment of collective learning, validating storytelling as a way to express change that happens to an individual or community over time."

Lezlie Wagman, SMART Fund, Vancouver Coastal Health

Sharing Inner Work

Every day, there are more people embracing and championing inner work tools and approaches. It is as if this way of working is coming out of the closet. I hope you will join me and many others in making inner work part of every household, work place, and community gathering.

To begin with, I hope you will tune in to your inner knowing on a regular basis. The more of us who are working in this way, the easier it is for others to access their inner knowing.

If you want to do more, here are some ideas:

- Let others know about inner work – in your personal life, at work, and in your community connections.

- Listen for and honour the inner knowing of children and youth. Do the same for friends, associates, and colleagues whose ways of knowing are intuitive or non-linear.

- If you work in an office or team, introduce inner work approaches into meetings and decision-making processes. Integrate the tools into your curricula if you are a teacher or instructor. Share inner work approaches with people in major transition if you are a parent, social worker, real estate agent, community worker, etc. Tune in about how best you can share inner work with others.

- Share your stories. What are your experiences using inner work? We draw inspiration and courage from hearing what others are doing. One story-sharing option is to contribute to the Make Light Work blog at www.katersutherland.com.

- Form a six week (or longer) support circle to help yourself and others integrate inner work into daily life. Check out PeerSpirit and Be The Change Earth Alliance for excellent resources on forming circles.

- Share other ideas for making inner work universally accessible, in your networks, and with Kate (kate@katersutherland.com, or 604-838-1408).

Together we can make light work.